RESOULUTIONS:
A Practical Guide for Self-Repair

by Rabbi Heather Miller

ISBN 978-1-300-79320-5

Cover design, Grace Ming

Project Editor, Rabbi Beth Lieberman

Excerpts from Babylonian Talmud Yoma 35b,
Babylonian Talmud Menachot 44a, and
Babylonian Talmud Taanit 23a reprinted from the
Koren Talmud Bavli (Adin Steinsalz, ed.). Used
with permission.

Dedication

This book is dedicated to all who enjoyed my
Omer Count passages on social media and
encouraged me to share these kinds of daily
writings. For you, I pulled Jewish wisdom from the
vaults to make it relevant in today's world. All my
love to my family, my beloved wife and our
children for their unwavering devotion. Endless
gratitude to my dearest of friends, especially my
Wellesley network and friends of faith, who have
helped me birth this work by encouraging
expression of these understandings of Torah. Many
thanks to my grandmother, who taught me how to
delight in Torah study, and to my mother and God
for creating and supporting me.

Table of Contents

Introduction

Encouraging Metamorphosis

Claiming Space

Redefining Challenge

Expanding Relationships

Introduction

I have always regarded the month of Elul as the secular month of December. It is the last month of the calendar year before the New Year. And, just as we reflect on our lives and prepare ourselves to make new year's resolutions in the secular year, the Jewish New Year calls us to reflect upon our lives and resolve to improve as well. The month of Elul is a heightened time to do this sacred work.

I wrote this book as a guide to help individuals reflect upon their past year and begin a process of transformation— for good. It pulls from Torah, which is the sacred literature of the Jewish people, across the ancient, medieval, and modern eras. Nevertheless, it resonates with relevance to the universal human experience. You may use it each of the 29 days of the month of Elul before the Jewish New Year of Rosh HaShanah, during the month of December before the secular New Year, or anytime, really. May it bring you many blessings.

Encouraging Metamorphosis

Day 1: The Universe Is Rooting for Your Growth

רבי סימון אין לך כל עשב ועשב,
שאין לו ברקיע שמכה אותו.

Rabbi Simon says: "There is not a single blade of
grass that doesn't have a mazal that is over it
encouraging it to grow."
– Genesis Rabbah 10:6

Some say this "*mazal*" is a body from the celestial
world, like the stars or supernatural forces, and
some envision the *mazal* to be an angel bent over
the blades of grass encouraging, "Grow! Grow!"

In either case, what we should take away from this
image is that each of us, like each blade of grass,
are encouraged to grow—to spend time improving
our faults and to expand the limits of who we are
in the present moment. It is a profound statement
to realize that the cosmic universe is encouraging
us each to transform into something better than we
are today.

As we enter into this season of *cheshbon hanefesh*,
the season of the accounting of our souls, we
should do so with a positive valence. We should
approach this season with an awareness that it is a
blessing that humans are able to improve, and
remain confident that this task is noble and
praiseworthy—the universe is rooting for us. This
is not a time of denigrating self-flagellation; rather
it is a time of growth and earnest commitment to
make for ourselves a brighter future.

Practice
- Take a moment to give thanks for the chance to improve.
- Boldly call to mind both areas of personal success and areas of challenge from the past year.
- What events are to be celebrated? What behaviors need to be addressed?

Blessed are You, Creator of the Universe who has given me life, sustained me, and brought me to this sacred time.

May you be blessed on your journey over the next 28 days...

Day 2: Torah Promotes Love

בת קול ואמרה להם, להחריב עולמי?
A Heavenly voice came out and said to them,
"Are you intending to destroy my world?"
– Babylonian Talmud, Shabbat 33b

In the Talmud, we learn about Rabbi Shimon bar Yohai who retreated into a cave with his son for twelve years to escape the Roman decree to punish anyone who would teach Torah. There, they buried themselves in sand up to their necks and studied Torah for hours and hours everyday, sustained only by a singular carob tree and the Divine light of Torah.

When the Roman decree was annulled and they were able to once again teach Torah, they emerged. However, their Torah knowledge was so potent that everywhere they would look, lasers would emerge from their eyes and they would destroy everyone and everything they would encounter. Suddenly, a Divine Voice revealed itself by asking a rhetorical question in order to correct their behavior: "Do you intend to destroy my world with Torah?" At that moment, they returned to the cave to study more and to temper the fierce judgment of the world that often comes with punctilious learning the laws of Torah.

The idea is that though the Torah is filled with ideas for living a meaningful life, and strictly adhering to them may incline one to judge oneself and others harshly. The heart of Torah study should never be used as a destructive force. Instead, Torah should be used as a generative tool of positivity and improvement.

So, even though self-examination of behaviors of the past year might incline a person toward critical self-analysis, one should not go overboard and self-flagellate. Be kind to yourself. The gift of the New Year is around the corner, and the chance to make it good, positive, and productive is nearing. Love yourself as the Divinely inspired creation that you are, always on the path of continued improvement.

Practice
• Write a list of the actions from the past year that you seek to improve in the year ahead.
• Balance that with a list of actions you're proud of from this past year that you hope to continue in the year ahead.
• Express gratitude for the ability to introspect.

Blessed are You, Creator of the Universe, who has given me the ability to distinguish between the sacred and the ordinary.

May you be blessed on your journey over the next 27 days...

Day 3: Torah Gives Life

עלה ונתלה וישב על פי ארובה כדי שישמע דברי
אלהים חיים מפי שמעיה באבטליון.

He ascended the roof, suspended himself, and sat
at the edge of the skylight in order to hear the
words of the Torah of the living God from the
months of Shemaya and Avtalyon, the spiritual
leaders of that generation.
– Babylonian Talmud, Yoma 35b

Another story to emphasize that the words of
Torah are always to be used to create, sustain and
preserve life is about Hillel the Elder found in the
Babylonian Talmud. When he was a youth, Hillel
would work and scrape together a few coins to
learn Torah from the mouths of the great teachers
of his day named Shemayah and Avtalyon. Once,
when he didn't have enough money to pay the
guard to let him in to study, he climbed up onto the
roof of the study hall to eavesdrop and hear Torah
coming from the mouths of the teachers. The
Torah that would come from their mouths was
described as the words of the Living God. Their
teachings were alive and life-giving, and sourced
from God who loves life.

Ironically, it was snowing that night and in the
morning, which happened to be the day of rest
known as Shabbat, the sages looked up and
realized that though it was daylight, their window
was darkened. They ascended the roof to
investigate and found a frozen Hillel there slumped
over the skylight. Though it would have

technically been against Jewish law to light a fire on Shabbat, they realized that Torah, especially the living words of Torah, are meant to preserve and save life, not condemn it. Since lighting a fire would be done in order to save life, they immediately sprang into action to save Hillel by building a fire and rubbing him with warm oils. We learn from this text that even the precepts and dictums of Torah must yield to saving life.

Practice
• Have you been using Torah to give life or to destroy it?
• How can you increase life-giving Torah study and practice in your life?
• How can it deepen your life experience giving you meaning and purpose rather than using it as a weapon against others' perceived practices?

Blessed are You, Creator of the Universe, who has inclined me to use my power for the good.

May you be blessed on your journey over the next 26 days...

Day 4: Taking On New Names

ויאמר לא יעקב יאמר עוד שמך, כי אם ישראל,
כי שרית עם אלהים ועם אנשים ותוכל.
"Your name shall no longer be Jacob, but Israel
since you have striven with God and with humans,
and have prevailed."
– Genesis 32:29

After Jacob, a homebody, stole the blessing meant
for his older brother Esau, a skilled hunter, he fled
for his life. He was on the run and came to a place
of remorse, perhaps inspired by mortal fear of God
and of his brother whom he had wronged. The
night before he would encounter his brother and
face the victim of the wrong he committed, he
wrestled with a being who renamed him and gave
him a blessing. Because the Torah doesn't name
the being, the ancient Sages suggest that the being
was the Divine. Some think it was an angel, while
others posit that it may have been his brother Esau,
or even himself. Either way, the story indicates that
some past behaviors may weigh so heavy on one's
heart that a major shift is necessary. A name
change symbolizes a change of one's entire
identity.

Self-acknowledgment of such a shift is only the
first step. Often, the harder part is then revealing to
others your own awareness of how you have
changed. Think of those who are released from jail,
but are constantly reminded of their past offenses
even though they have changed. Or those who
come out as queer or genderqueer or trans. Or

those who have changed careers, or changed marital status. These are profound shifts that often come with a literal name or title change.

But other shifts such as a major medical diagnosis, becoming a parent, or losing a child, a discovery of the deeper self as revealed in therapy, or the experience of a traumatic event can feel just as impactful. Some transformations call for this larger leap from who we are to who we are meant to become.

For those of us who need to affirm a fundamental shift in who we are, we can look for inspiration to the story of Jacob wrestling and the blessed name change he experienced. Some years a fundamental transformation of this magnitude is called for—and as is suggested in the *Book of Genesis,* this type of metamorphosis is a blessing.

Practice

• Do any major shifts in your life call for a shift in one's identity, such that a name change would be necessary?

• Have you been able to acknowledge these kinds of major shifts in your life? Have you been able to change your name or reputation in the process and communicate the change to those around you?

• How might you recognize how others may have changed as well, and dignify their profound growth?

Blessed are You, Creator of the Universe, who has given me a deep, complex, beautiful, and wondrous essence to express in the world.

May you be blessed on your journey over the next 25 days...

Day 5: Looking to the Margins

ואלמנה ויתום גר ועני אל תעשקו.

Do not oppress the widow, the orphan,
the stranger, or the poor.
— Zechariah 7:10

Self-inventory must be comprehensive. One should
consider one's actions not only toward the great
and powerful, but also the interactions we have
with those on the margins. Jewish sacred literature
often instructs us to consider the widow, orphan,
stranger and poor as a way to remind us that
morality should not only be extended to the mighty
but to all of humanity. The *Books of Zechariah,
Malachi, Isaiah, Deuteronomy, Exodus, Psalms,
Jeremiah* and countless rabbinic works stress the
importance of holding the powerless in equal
esteem as others to dignify their existence and
bring about justice. They should rejoice with us,
and be provided with food, clothing and shelter.

Deuteronomy even says that by considering the
stranger and providing for them in these ways, the
stranger and widow and orphan become a blessing
to us.

In society today, we can consider the treatment of
the lowest paid worker in companies especially
relative to the top-paid CEO. We can consider how
well we tip servers and those who clean our hotel
rooms. We can consider how we treat orphans and
widows and strangers, particularly immigrants,
recently emancipated youth, and women without

17

agency in our communities. When we do provide for their well-being, they can express their talents, skills, and strengths and truly become a blessing.

Practice
• Who is on the margins that you need to pay more attention to? Whose voice is left out of your conversation?
• How are those on the margins treated in your community, in your neighborhood, in the country, and in the world?
• How can you lift up their voices, amplify them or, better yet, bring them into the room where decisions are being made and support them there, to give voice to their perspective for themselves, in the coming year?

Blessed are You, Creator of the Universe, who created each person different from the next yet infuses each with Your essence.

May you be blessed on your journey over the next 24 days...

Day 6: Becoming Who You are Meant to Be

אמרה ליה זיל הוי בי רב אזל תרתי סרי
שנין קמי דר׳ אליעזר ור׳ יהושע.

She said to him:,"Go and become the great one
who you are meant to be!" He went and sharpened
his mind among the great teachers Rabbi Eliezer
and Rabbi Joshua for twelve years.
— Babylonian Talmud Nedarim 50a; also found in
Ketubot 62b and Gittin 56a

Perhaps the rabbinic sage who underwent the
greatest personal and public transformation was
Rabbi Akiva. The *Talmud* tells us, in three places,
that he began his life as a poor shepherd for a
wealthy Jerusalemite named Ben Kalba Savua.
When he and Ben Kalba Savua's daughter fell in
love and got married, they were both disinherited
because Kalba Savua didn't approve. At the age of
40, he told his wife that he desired learning Torah,
and with her blessing, he went away to study for
12 years. Remarkably, just has he was returning to
town after such a long time away, he overheard a
curmudgeon neighbor cursing him to his wife,
"Look, your husband left you for dead while he
was off jauntily studying!" She replied, "If it were
up to me, Akiva would enjoy another 12 years
studying!" Well, Akiva took that as a directive and
turned around and went to study another 12 years.

Finally, when he returned to town, he did so with
24,000 students. He was a great and renowned

man, unrecognizable to the townspeople. When his wife approached his entourage entering the city, the townspeople berated her and pushed her away. But Rabbi Akiva recognized his wife, and gave her credit for his transformation: "My Torah knowledge and yours is actually because of her!"

This story conveys several lessons. First, the fact that Akiva was able to name what he wanted to pursue reminds us that getting in touch with what our soul is calling us to do and become is an essential first step. Second, the fact that Akiva began his studies at age 40 teaches us that it is never too late to become who we were meant to be. Third, the fact that his wife supported his commitment to his self-improvement teaches us that it is critical to surround ourselves with supporters. Fourth, the fact that Rabbi Akiva and his wife didn't let her father or their neighbor divert their attention from their destiny reminds us to attune ourselves to our destiny and ignore the haters. And fifth, their perseverance reminds us to make sure that when we decide to pursue a dream, we really follow through and pursue it.

Practice
• Have you yet begun to name and claim your soul's desire, regardless of your stage of life?
• Have you shared this among your innermost circle of supporters and thereby gained strength to ignore any naysayers?
• Have you begun to take serious steps towards fulfilling your own potential?

Blessed are You, Creator of the Universe, who created me in Your image.

May you be blessed on your journey over the next 23 days...

Day 7: Uncovering Your Truths

כי אם החרש תחרישי בעת הזאת, רוח והצלה יעמוד
ליהודים ממקום אחר, ואת ובית אביך תאבדו, ומי
יודע אם לעת כזאת הגעת למלכות.

"For if you remain silent now, it is possible that
relief and salvation will come to the Jews from
another place, while you and your father's house
will perish. Besides, who knows? Maybe you were
meant to arise to this royal position for precisely
such a time as this?"
– Esther 4:14

The book of Esther is the story of a woman coming
into her own strength and power. Esther becomes
the queen of Shushan, wife to a king named
Ahashverosh, though she does not reveal her
Jewish identity. During their marriage, the king is
convinced by his evil adviser to declare a date to
the exterminate all of the Jews of Shushan.
Esther's Uncle Mordecai encourages Esther to
reveal her Jewish identity to the king before the
date comes to pass in the hopes that she will be
able to convince him to annul his decree. He
persuades her to act by reminding her that she and
her family may never enjoy true safety if such a
decree comes to pass, and besides, perhaps she was
lifted into this royal position of access to power
precisely for this historic moment in time. With
this pep talk, she realizes that she is in a unique
position of influence and she can no longer hide
her identity— she must act to save her people.

When she reveals to the king that she is Jewish and asks him to cancel the decree, he does, and the Jews are saved.

This is a story about the importance of people revealing their true identity. It is about affirming who you are in your heart, sometimes with the encouragement of others, and then claiming your identity in the broader arena. Revealing who you are authentically invites God to work in the world through you because you are in touch with who you were created to be. And doing so is a blessing.

Practice
- Who helps you identify who you are at your essence? Who do you most feel yourself around?
- Who are you in those interactions that you are not able to reveal in other contexts?
- What would it look like to reveal your authentic self in a broader array of contexts, and claim your space?

Blessed are You, Creator of the Universe, who speaks the truth.

May you be blessed on your journey over the next 22 days…

Claiming Space

Day 8: Sanctifying Spaces

שֶׁכָּל זְמַן שֶׁשָּׂרָה קַיֶּמֶת, הָיָה נֵר דָּלוּק מֵעֶרֶב
לְעֶרֶב שַׁבָּת.
While Sarah was alive, a light had been burning in
the tent from one Shabbat evening to the next.
– Rashi on Genesis 24:67

Sarah was the first Jewish woman, and as such, the rabbis wondered what she might have done to define her life as such. Eleventh century French Rabbi Shlomo Ben Yitzchaki, also known as Rashi, comments that Sarah sanctified every Sabbath day by lighting candles. In doing so, she made room to hold space for rest and rejuvenation, praise and gratitude through ritual. She intuited the importance of making room for the holy amidst the monotonous days of the regular week. She brought light into the world by making space for it.

Whoever you are, wherever you are, you have the opportunity to sanctify space; to bring in a sense of the mystery and Divine connection, purpose and rootedness. Some may do this through ritual. For example, beloveds sometimes declare space under the *chuppah* as holy by circling one another. Others usher in a sense of the sacred in our own lives through moments of sharing the depths of pivotal experiences with new friends, perpetuating stellar sportsmanlike conduct during a ball game, by stopping to appreciate the pure beauty of nature on a hike, or sharing a raw story of injustice during a rally in order to inspire positive action. We each

25

have the ability to imbue otherwise mundane moments with sacredness.

Practice
- How and where do you claim your space in the world, where you reveal your deepest truths?
- What spaces do you create for others to feel supported in their sacred sharing?
- What is to be gained from punctuating life with the holding of sacred space?

Blessed are You, Creator of the Universe, who dwells in the world among us.

May you be blessed on your journey over the next 21 days...

Day 9: Leaving the Comforts of Home

ויאמר ה׳ אל אברם, לך לך מארצך וממולדתך ומבית
אביך, אל הארץ אשר אראך.

Adonai said to Avram, "Go forth from your native
land, and from your father's house, to the land that
I will show you."
– Genesis 12:1

Abraham is famous for being the first Jew. Or,
actually, the first monotheist. But when he was a
youth and still known by the name Avram, God
first called him to depart from all that he knew. All
that was familiar to him. From his father's house.
From his native land, from his old self toward his
new being.

The first two words of Genesis 12:1 are "*lech
lecha*" which is often translated as "Go forth." But
literally, it means "Go to yourself." You see, the
Torah reveals here that to become yourself and
move toward who you are meant to be requires a
bold commitment to depart from who you have
been. To claim new space requires a departure of
old space.

Practice
• What is holding you back from becoming
yourself in the world?
• What might you have to let go of or leave behind,
not irresponsibly but rather with intention, to
become?
• How might you step into your own essence?

Blessed are You, Creator of the Universe, who travels with us.

May you be blessed on your journey over the next 20 days…

Day 10: The Truly Eternal

קוֹל אֹמֵר קְרָא וְאָמַר מָה אֶקְרָא כָּל הַבָּשָׂר

חָצִיר וְכָל חַסְדּוֹ כְּצִיץ הַשָּׂדֶה.

יָבֵשׁ חָצִיר נָבֵל צִיץ כִּי רוּחַ יְהוָה

נָשְׁבָה בּוֹ אָכֵן חָצִיר הָעָם.

A voice says, "Call out!" And he says, "What shall
I proclaim?" "All flesh is grass, and all its
goodness is like the flower of the field. The grass
withers, the flower fades because the breath of God
blows on it; surely the people are grass."
– Isaiah 40:6-7

This passage of text is often recited at the gravesite
of a funeral as it reminds us that every living being
is part of the cycle of life. Like grass, we all grow
and fade, wither and die. We each have an
expiration date.

For this reason, the text is also read during Shabbat
Nachamu, the Shabbat of Consolation. This is the
special Shabbat that occurs immediately following
Av, the commemoration of the Tisha B
destruction of the Temple. And as such, it reminds
us that not only is life fleeting, but so, too, are
institutions. Physical houses of worship and human
bodies are both sacred homes housing the
intangible. But it is the intangible, the essence, is
that which is truly Eternal.

This text reminds us to get in touch with what is
sacred and pure and everlasting about ourselves.
We remember that claiming space is not about

physically man-spreading or puffing our our chests or being a bull in a china shop to stretch out and claim physical space. Rather, it is about being intentional about the mark we want to leave on the world; it is about claiming our space on the great timeline of human existence.

Practice
• For what do we want to be remembered?
• What do we consider core to our existence?
• How do we claim space in the name of that intangible value?

Blessed are You, Creator of the Universe, Source of life, Guardian of memory.

May you be blessed on your journey over the next 19 days…

Day 11: Standing Up for Others

ויהי בימים ההם, ויגדל משה ויצא אל אחיו, וירא
בסולותם. וירא איש מצרי מכה איש עברי מאחיו.

Later, when Moses was grown up, he went out
unto his brothers, and looked on their burdens; and
he saw an Egyptian hitting a Hebrew, one of his
brothers.

– Exodus 2:11

It is a human need to become who we are supposed
to be, but there is often a strong impulse to provide
others with the room to be fully themselves as
well. In his early years, Moses witnessed the labors
of the Hebrews under the rule of the cruel Pharaoh.
They were whipped and beaten and forced to work
in the harshest of weather conditions. They were
oppressed and it disgusted him. Once, when he
witnessed an Egyptian taskmaster acting
particularly cruelly to one of the Hebrew slaves,
Moses rose up and stopped the behavior by killing
the taskmaster. This action of standing up against
injustice is what gave him the experience to
eventually stand up to Pharaoh's oppressive ways.

Truly holding space for the sacred means not only
cultivating room for the sacred and preserving
one's own dignity, but it also extends to
safeguarding the dignity of others. At times, each
of us is called to take a stand no matter the risk to
personal liberty. As the *Book of Deuteronomy*
commands, "Justice, justice you shall pursue." We
must work toward justice for all.

Some may do this through direct actions like protests and sit-ins, others through voter engagement and advocacy, others by addressing the issues from within powerful institutions, or still others by re-imagining the way things ought to be and working for that new vision. Truly holding sacred space means recognizing that we are all profoundly connected, and working for the dignity of all.

Practice
• How have you affirmed your human dignity and that of others?
• Whose dignity is most threatened in your sphere of influence, and what can you do to uplift them and amplify their voices?
• How can you affirm others' claiming of their sacred space?

Blessed are You, Creator of the Universe, who gives strength to those who stand up for dignity.

May you be blessed on your journey over the next 18 days…

Day 12: Carpe Diem

She drew near to the bed, took hold of the hair of
his head, and said, "Strengthen me, O Lord God of
Israel, this day." She struck twice upon his neck
with all her might, and took away his head from
him.
– Judith 13:7-8

The miracle of Hanukkah is not only attributed to
the might of the Maccabees who overcame the
fierce Assyrian army who had plundered and
defiled the Temple. The matriarch Judith also
played a critical role in defeating the Assyrian
army as well. In the deuterocanonical work known
as The Book of Judith, Judith feeds the Assyrian
general named Holofernes copious amounts of
salty cheese to get him thirsty for wine.
Predictably, he passes out providing her with the
opportunity to behead the military leader. When
his severed head was revealed the next morning,
his troops were so distraught that they could not
muster the mindset nor strength to fight, thus
securing the Maccabean victory.

Part of claiming space relies on both knowing your
skill set, and seizing opportunities presented to
you.

Practice
• What unique tools do you possess?
• How can you use them for good?

- What opportunities are lying at your feet and what would it take for you to step in and claim that space for the sake of goodness?

Blessed are You, Creator of the Universe, who girds humanity with heroism.

May you be blessed on your journey over the next 17 days...

Day 13: Strength and Courage

חֲזַק וֶאֱמָץ.
Be strong and courageous.
– Deuteronomy 31:7

Be strong and courageous" repeats "The phrase, several times in the Tanakh. When we think about claiming our own space and claiming space for others, we must acknowledge that it is a continual process, not just a singular action. Claiming space often requires a claim and then a holding of that space to protect it from the outside. Whether that is claiming a sacred relationship and guarding that from intruders, claiming market space across s truth in ʾdigital platforms, or standing up for one social circles, we know that the claiming of space requires strength and courage to hold a line. Rebbe Nachman of Breslov, the 18th century founder of Hasidic Judaism, notes that one needs to be strong and courageous when facing those who aim to tear you down.

Practice
• What space have you needed to hold this past year?
• What has threatened to erode those boundaries?
• How might you demonstrate strength and courage in your holding of that space in the next year?

Blessed are You, Creator of the Universe, who allows humanity to access wellsprings of strength and courage.

May you be blessed on your journey over the next 16 days…

Day 14: Sweet Talk

אֲנִי לְדוֹדִי וְדוֹדִי לִי.

I am my beloved's and my beloved is mine.
– Song of Songs 6:3

Creating sacred space requires a bold claiming of
space and a fierce commitment to hold that space.
But, the claiming of space can also involve sweetly
and pleasantly taking an otherwise mundane
interaction and elevating it though tender speech.
This invites others to help create, claim and hold
the sacred space as well.

The Song of Songs is a unique genre of biblical
literature—it is by and large one epic ancient love
poem. In it, the author shares sensual readings
about the beauty of love and relationship. It can
sometimes feel uncomfortable to read, as it is a
sensuous description by one beloved to the other
about their desirable qualities—both spiritual and
physical. While it feels almost voyeuristic to read
because it is so intimate, it also serves to remind us
of the importance of reminding our loved ones, our
romantic partners, and our platonic partners as well
of the importance of expressing love and
appreciation to infuse holiness into the
relationship.

We may do this through a well-placed and sincere,
"Thank You." Or, through a love note. We may do
this though a thoughtful gesture, a gift, or a kind
consideration. The more tailored to the other's
particularities, the better.

Practice
- Who is deserving of your demonstration of love and loyalty?
- When was the last time you claimed space to express love and appreciation toward this person?
- How might you resolve to infuse kind words and appreciation into the relationship moving forward?

Blessed are You, Creator of the Universe, Source of sweet language.

May you be blessed on your journey over the next 15 days...

Redefining Challenge

Day 15: Returning to Your Best Self

וישלחהו ח' אלהים מגן עדן.

Therefore Adonai sent him out from the
Garden of Eden.
– Genesis 3:23

The first human beings, Adam and Eve, were
kicked out of the Garden of Eden. Some say it was
because they each ate from the Tree of Life. But
the Midrash (*Genesis Rabbah 21:6*) imagines that
it was actually not because of the transgression of
eating from the tree—rather it was because Adam
refused to repent for having done so.

You see, when the world was created, so, too was
the Jewish concept of *teshuvah*: repentance.
Literally, the term *teshuvah* means "return." The
concept is that repentance is a reset for the times
when we stray from the path of being the best
person we could be by doing something erroneous;
teshuvah returns us to our best selves. *Teshuvah*
often takes the form of a verbal apology,
commitment to not make the mistake again, and
even some sort of justice in terms of monetary or
material recompense. The Jewish High Holy Days
are all about this type of introspection of past
missteps, and the work of return to being the best
person one can be in the new year. Humans have
been making mistakes since we were created.
Mistakes are to be expected. They key is to address
this fact by partnering with God in the creation of
the world, to help restore it to the perfection
experienced in the Garden of Eden, by utilizing the

process of *teshuvah* to right our wrongs. We can't experience the peace and tranquility we experienced in the Garden of Eden without utilizing the gift of *teshuvah*.

Practice
• What mistakes have you made this year that have kept you from expressing your best self? What consequences have come from that behavior or action?
• What might teshuvah look like?
• How might it feel to restore that little piece of the world to that kind of perfection through teshuvah?

Blessed are You, Creator of the Universe, who forgives us so that we may be forgiven.

May you be blessed on your journey over the next 14 days...

Day 16: Self-Awareness Brings Blessing

באו ד׳ ציציותיו וטפחו לו על פניו.
In the meantime, his four ritual fringes came and
slapped him on his face.
– Babylonian Talmud, Menachot 44a

Okay, so this is quite an interesting story in the
Talmud. It begins with a man who heard about a
prostitute who charged the large sum of 400 gold
coins for her services. The man wondered what
incredible experience could be worth 400 gold
coins.

He let his curiosity get the best of him, and he
sought out this prostitute. He found her
maidservant and paid the 400 gold coins. He was
led into a chamber consisting of a tower of six
silver beds stacked on top of one another and at the
top was a seventh bed made of gold on top of
which sat the beautiful, naked, prostitute. Ladders
connected the beds. He began to climb up to her.
As he was undressing to join her in nakedness, a
funny thing happened: the fringes of his tallit (his
prayer shawl) smacked him in the face. At that
moment he awoke from his lascivious desires, and
descended the ladders to leave.

"Wait a minute!" she demanded. "I have to
know—what's wrong with me?!"

He then explained to her that nothing was wrong
with her—it was just that the fringes on his tallit
reminded him of the commandments, and

ultimately having to answer to God for his behaviors. And so, he couldn't proceed. To say she was impressed was an understatement. She decided to convert to Judaism, and eventually, she married the man.

From this story we learn that it is never too late to turn back from doing something that one will later regret. One may even be rewarded in unexpected ways for doing so. Humans will make mistakes. But the ways we respond to them, even if in the midst of transgressing, and the ways that we think about them later on, create our reality. The rabbis encourage each of us to never think of ourselves or our behavior as a lost cause. To never think it is too late to begin *teshuvah*, and to be motivated by the idea that there may be untold and surprising rewards for sincere *teshuvah*.

Practice
• Are you currently engaged in activities of which you are not proud?
• How might you resolve to transform your behavior to become something of which you are proud and change the story you're writing for yourself?
• The man had his tallit fringes to help keep him focused on the importance of his behaviors: what physical reminder might help you to make decisions you're proud of? Fringes? A bracelet or necklace of significance? Something else?

Blessed are You, Creator of the Universe, who has given us wisdom to distinguish between day and night, blessing and transgression.

May you be blessed on your journey over the next 13 days...

Day 17: Radical Reconciliation

ויתן את קולו בבכי, וישמעו מצרים,
וישמע בית פרעה.

He sobbed aloud; and the Egyptians heard, and the
house of Pharaoh heard.
– Genesis 45:2

Across the four Torah portions concluding the
book of Genesis, we learn of the story of Joseph.
When he was a youth, his 11 brothers threw him
into a pit in the middle of the desert and left him
for dead. From there, Joseph was picked up by
traveling merchants and sold into slavery. Some
time later, he was accused of trying to seduce his
master's wife, and thrown in jail. There, he became
a masterful interpreter of dreams, and
demonstrated his skill for the Pharaoh who
appointed him his chief advisor. He correctly
predicted a famine and outlined a plan for Egypt to
survive.

During the famine, Joseph's brothers travelled a
great distance, desperate for refuge in Egypt.
Ironically, they came to appear before Joseph to
plead their case, but, because so many years had
passed and because of his new station in the
kingdom, they didn't recognize him. At first, he
dealt with them harshly and orchestrated a
complex plot to test them to see if they would
abandon his full blood brother, Benjamin, as they
had so easily betrayed him so many years prior.
Instead, they risk their own lives for their brother,
and he realizes that they have truly changed. He is

moved by their obvious transformation. Then and there, he dramatically reveals his true identity to them. The text describes his deep cathartic release as he hugs them and sobs with cries so loud that all of Egypt, including Pharaoh, could hear them. This reconciliation and the resulting granting of refuge brings about an eventual prosperity for the entire family.

We learn from this story that no matter how many years have gone by, *teshuvah* is possible. It can be profound, and it can be a blessing.

Practice
• Thinking back on the years of your life, are there deep regrets that haunt you?
• What would it look like to address the source of those regrets?
• What tests would have to be engaged before you felt safe enough to ask for forgiveness or grant forgiveness? And if it's not possible, how might you make peace living with this unease?

Blessed are You, Creator of the Universe, who allows humanity the expression of emotion when words fail us.

May you be blessed on your journey over the next 12 days…

Day 18: The King Has Returned

הקריבה לפניו המאכל ואכל ובירך, לאחר שבירך
אמרה לו 'רבי, שאלה אחת יש לי לשאול לך,'
אמר לה 'אמרי שאלתך.'

She placed food in front of him and he ate and
blessed. After he blessed, she said to him, "I have a
question to ask you." He said to her, "Say your
question."

– Midrash Proverbs 31:2

Midrash tells a story about Rabbi Meir, his wife
Beruriah, and their twin sons. One day, Rabbi Meir
went out to the synagogue to pray. While he was
there, their twin sons died unexpectedly. Beruriah
discovered their deaths and lovingly laid their
bodies on the bed and placed a single sheet over
their bodies. Then, amidst her grief, she came up
with a plan of how to inform her husband of their
devastating losses. When he returned home, he
inquired as to the whereabouts of their sons. In
turn, she asked if he'd like some food, and then
proceeded to tell him a parable.

"If a king were to come by and ask us to safeguard
two precious rubies for some time, and then later
came to claim them, should we give them back to
the king?"

"Who is asking for two rubies back from us?" Meir
said.

She then led him into the room and pulled back the sheet.

Beruriah was reputed to have been learned, and very wise. This story conveys her frame of mind at the deaths of her two sons. She displayed an almost super-human mindset at the tragic reality in front of her. Her frame was that her sons were never truly hers— that they were rather two precious jewels placed into her care by God, and that for whatever reason, God had come to reclaim them that day.

The point here is not that our children are not truly ours, or that this doesn't present theological problems as to why God would want to claim children before their parents. Rather, it reminds us that we truly are in charge of the way we frame the tragedies that we experience in life. That if we look for a narrative of being tortured or forsaken, as could have been the frame for Beruriah, we could have resorted into self-destruction. The key is to look for the frame that will help us to be strengthened in the future. When things happen to us, pay attention to the frame—the frame is everything.

Practice
• What major loss did you endure this year?
• How do you understand it?
• What frame would be one that would help to strengthen you rather than defeat you?

Blessed are You, Creator of the Universe, who opens the eyes of the blind, expanding our perception of reality.

May you be blessed on your journey over the next 11 days...

Day 19: Life Cycles

אי זו היא תשובה גמורה? זה שבא לידו דבר שעבר
בו, ואפשר בידו לעשותו.
ופרש ולא עשה מפני התשובה.

What is complete repentance? When a person is
placed again in the same situation where before
they had committed a sin, but now do not repeat
the violation because of teshuvah, and not out of
fear or lack of strength.
– Mishneh Torah Hilchot Teshuvah 2:1

Life cycles. You may feel yourself returning and
returning again to the same spots. The same
archetypes of characters leave your life and return
again. You may feel *deja vu*. New loves remind
you of past loves. New threats remind you of old
threats. We get chances to return and return again
to who we are and how we engage in situations.

This occurs generationally, too. The Torah
(Genesis 26:18) reminds us that Isaac re-dug wells
that his father Abraham had dug in his day.
Sociologically we know that fortune and
misfortune and our responses to it has a way of
cycling through families. The study of epigenetics
suggests that deep psychological memories of our
forebears has a way of imprinting themselves on
our DNA, giving us visceral reactions to stimuli.

One way to approach these cycles of life is to
embrace them for the new opportunities they
provide. They become chances to break negative

cycles that do not serve the world, or serve our souls. If you pause to recognize your strong responses to certain people, and you probe your subconscious for the patterns and archetypes they may represent in your life, you may begin to recognize the cycles. And from there—you may, with effort, break them.

Practice
- Who in your life do you respond strongly to?
- What are the qualities they share with past figures in your life?
- How will this realization serve you as you continue to engage with them in the future?

Blessed are You, Creator of the Universe, who made us to seek freedom from that which entraps us.

May you be blessed on your journey over the next 10 days...

Day 20: Spiritual Movement

At the conclusion of the seventh day of mourning,
the period known as shiva, the mourners should get
up from the house of mourning and walk around
the block accompanied by their community.
– Jewish Custom

The custom of walking around the block at the
conclusion of the seventh day of mourning is a
beautiful way that movement through time and
space can encourage movement through grief.
Getting up, getting out of the house and placing
one foot in front of the other, particularly
surrounded by community, provides the
opportunity to move through space and time to
transform the experience.

Just as emotional and spiritual grief manifests
physically in the body for many people, so too can
movement of the body influence and transform
emotional and spiritual grief. This is also why
running a 5k or marathon, volunteering to clean up
a natural habitat, or helping out in a public food
pantry in memory of a loved one can be so
healing.

Just as the mind/spirit/emotion/body connection
functions in grief, so, too, does it function in other
areas of the spirit. Similar connections may be
made towards repentance and other kinds of loss
and regret throughout the year.

Practice
- Where are you spiritually stuck in life?
- Have you only addressed your spiritual issues with spiritual or emotional activities?
- What physical activities would be safe for you to employ in the endeavor of spiritual or emotional transformation?

Blessed are You, Creator of the Universe, who makes firm each of our steps.

May you be blessed on your journey over the next
9 days...

Day 21: Bring the Brokenness with You

לוחות ושברי לוחות מונחות בארון.
The whole tablets and the broken tablets were
placed in the Ark.
– Babylonian Talmud, Berachot 8b

Torah tells us that Moses ascended Mount Sinai to
receive the two tablets of stone on which the ten
commandments were written. But when he
descended the mountain, he found the people
engaged in the sin of worshipping the image of a
calf that they had hewn from gold. He became
enraged and broke the two tablets and eventually
re-ascended the mountain and came down with a
new set of tablets.

The Babylonian Talmud reveals that both the
whole and the broken tablets were carried in the
ark by the Israelites everywhere they traveled.
Society encourages us to embody perfection, but
here, we see that the Jewish tradition regards both
the whole and the broken as sacred. They are
carried together on the continued journeys of the
people.

This means that the human experiences of loss,
grief, and heartbreak should be regarded as sacred
and should not be cast off. They continue along
with us, some would say, as "baggage." But sacred
baggage. These are the experiences that help make
us who we are, and if we are lucky, they have
provided us with wisdom about ourselves and
about life.

Practice
• What brokenness are you carrying with you?
• Have you been trying to deny, ignore or cast it off?
• What would it be like to sit with it and acknowledge that you carry it with you, but that it doesn't have to weigh you down?

Blessed are You, Creator of the Universe, who cherishes the whole and the broken.

May you be blessed on your journey over the next 8 days...

Expanding Relationship

Day 22: Finding Yourself Responsible

הלוקה פירות מחברו או ששלחלו חברו פירות, ומצא
בהן מעות, הרי אלו שלו.
אם היו צרורין, נוטל ומכריז.

If a man bought fruit from his fellow or if his
fellow sent him fruit and he found coins therein,
they belong to him. But if they were tied up he
must take them and proclaim them.
– Mishnah Bava Metzia 2:4

In life, it is easy to get caught up in the grind of
self-centeredness and greed. It is easy to be
singularly focused on acquiring for the benefit of
oneself no matter the cost to others. But there is a
large section of Jewish ethical law dedicated to
helping humans think about expanding our
understanding of responsibility. For example, tort
laws found in the Mishnah remind us that there is
some responsibility when a person finds money on
the street. We are responsible for returning the
property of those in our community.

The Talmud affirms that each person in the
community is responsible for one another. We are
more than just ourselves in this world, and as we
move forward, it is important to take time to
expand our own awareness of our circles of
responsibility.

Practice
• For whom, beyond yourself, are you responsible? How have you demonstrated taking responsibility for them?
• If you were to expand that circle, who would you include?
• How might you include them in your consciousness as you live and act in the world?

Blessed are You, Creator of the Universe, who blessed us with both the joys and responsibilities of community.

May you be blessed on your journey over the next 7 days...

Day 23: Taking a Chance on Love

ויקראו לרבקה ויאמרו אליה, התלכי עם האיש הזה,
ותאמר אלך.

They called Rebekah and said to her, "Will you go
with this man?" And she said, "I will."
– Genesis 24:58

When Rebekah was about 40 years old, a man
approached her in the desert as she was drawing
water from her family's well. He had been
traveling and was thirsty. Being a kind person, she
naturally asked if she could draw water for him
and his 10 camels, which he readily accepted. She
took him back to her family tent and her family
invited him to stay with them for the night.

After dinner, he told them of a fantastic story,
revealing that he was a servant and his master,
Abraham, had sent him on a mission to find a wife
for his master's son, Isaac. He surmised that he
would know the person by her kindness at offering
to give water to him and his 10 camels. This is
exactly what Rebekah did, and so, the servant
wanted to know if Rebekah would go with him to
meet Isaac. She paused for a moment and then she
uttered one word: "*Eilech*/I will go."

One word demonstrated how she was open to love,
even an unbelievable story such as that of the
servant. She would open her heart to the
possibilities.

Well, when she finally met Isaac, she fell off her camel, she was so taken with his presence. And, the rest is history. Love can also be incredible if we open ourselves to it. A tender heart is one open to human connection, and open to receiving the most beautiful gift of all: love.

Practice
• How have you closed yourself off from human connection this past year and why was that the way you operated?
• How might you consider safely opening yourself up to relationship this year?
• What might you lose? What might you gain?

Blessed are You, Creator of the Universe, who opens tender hearts to love.

May you be blessed on your journey over the next 6 days…

Day 24: Keep Working on Love

אמרה לו, מה הוא עושה מאותה שעה בעד עכשיו?
אמר לה, הקדוש ברוך הוא יושב ומזווג זווגים:
בתו פלוני לפלוני, אשתו של פלוני לפלוני,
ממונו של פלוני לפלוני.

"And since then, what has God been doing?" she
asked. R. Yosi replied, "God sits and makes
matches: the daughter of this one to that one, the
widow of this one to that one, the money of this
one to that one."
– Genesis Rabbah 68:4

A Roman once noticed that the Torah says that the
entire world was created in just six days. She posed
a difficult question to Rabbi Yosi. "Since then," she
asked, "what has God been doing?" Rabbi Yosi
replied that God has been matchmaking all this
time.

The lesson is that matchmaking is hard, even for
God who was powerful enough to create the entire
world in just six days. Finding people who can be
matched as great lovers or great friends or great
family members is difficult, even for the Divine.
All the more so for us, earthly human beings. But
since God keeps working at it, maybe we should,
too. We might find a new friend while cheering on
our child at a ball game, or we might resolve to
work on an issue in a friendship that has stalled or
suffered a rift. Working on relationships can be
emotionally, physically, mentally and spiritually
draining. However, sometimes everything aligns,

61

and from the effort, a significant, deep, meaningful, and long-lasting relationship forms. These are among the most fulfilling human experiences in life.

Practice
• How much perseverance have you dedicated toward the act of creating and maintaining meaningful relationships?
• What relationships have you abandoned, betrayed or neglected? How might you repair those relationships or take responsibility for your shortcomings?
• How might you cherish and value your relationships moving forward, and commit to dedicating energies towards them?

Blessed are You, Creator of the Universe, who seeks out love for all.

May you be blessed on your journey over the next 5 days...

Day 25: Jump into Your Future

מִי כָמֹכָה בָּאֵלִם ה'.
Who is like You among the mighty, O Adonai?
– Exodus 15:11

Pharaoh released the Israelites from slavery in
Egypt, but then he changed his mind. His troops
pursued them to attack from behind. As they fled
the fast-approaching army, they encountered a
huge roadblock before them— the Red Sea.
Realizing they were out of options and would
surely die there, they were bereft. Midrash tells us
that a man named Nachshon could not bear to let
the approaching army kill them there. So, he leapt
into the waters not knowing what would happen.

There, he found himself muttering, "Who is like
You O God?" His cries got louder and louder as he
continued into the waters and they began to
threaten his life. Still he pressed forward with a
stubborn hope beyond rational hope in his heart.
Eventually, when he was far enough into the sea
and the waters rose to cover his lips and nose and
he began choking on the words he was shouting,
miraculously, something dramatic happened. The
waters parted, revealing dry land upon which the
people would escape to freedom.

Nachshon freed his soul to replace the facts of
what was in front of him, with what could be. He
conquered his fears of sure death with his
imagination and relentless sense of hope. His
example may inspire us to try to imagine our way

out of a difficult or seemingly impossible situation before us.

Practice
• How are your perceptions about the limits of your life constraining you?
• What would it take for you to free your soul to imagine another way forward, no matter how fantastical?
• How might you open yourself to new possibilities and what steps would you need to take to make the seemingly impossible, possible?

Blessed are You, Creator of the Universe, who is awesome and powerful.

May you be blessed on your journey over the next 4 days...

Day 26: Lighting a Way for Others

ויאמר, מקל מהיותך לי עבד, להקים את שבטי יעקב,
ונצורי ישראל להשיב, ונתתיך לאור גויים,
להיות ישועתי עד קצה הארץ.

And God said, "It is too small a thing that you
should just be my servant to lift up the tribes of
Jacob and to restore the remainder of Israel; You
will be for Me a light to the nations, so that My
salvation reaches to the end of the earth."
– Isaiah 49:6

Isaiah reminds us that we should not confine our
light within ourselves, nor even just among our
own people. Rather, we should shine our light to
those around us to "be a light to the nations." Each
of our experiences, good and challenging, uplifting
and devastating, teaches lessons and sheds
perspectives. As we discover others who walk
similar paths, we might consider sharing our
experiences with them, to illumine the path we
have traveled, and to help them see more clearly
the path set out before them. Sharing within the
context of friendship, mentorship, camaraderie,
and partnership can all help those around us
achieve our collective greatest potential. To do
this, you may coach little league ball, volunteer
your expertise in certain areas through a job
training facility, reply to a hive mind request for
help on social media, or become active in a college
alumni network mentoring new graduates.
Whenever you pass along the wisdom, skills,
training and experience you have gained, you uplift

others around you and lighten the load of carrying their burden. And, as a result, we all shine.

Practice
• Think about your most significant setbacks and greatest triumphs: what have you learned from these experiences and who might benefit in hearing about your journey?
• How much time might you consider devoting to others' development and success?
• What might you, in turn, also learn in the process of sharing your story?

Blessed are You, Creator of the Universe, who gives us agency to positively impact upon generations to come.

May you be blessed on your journey over the next 3 days...

Day 27: Neighbor Care

מרחיקין את הסלם מן השובך ארבע אמות
כדי שלא תקפיץ הנמיה.

A person's ladder must not be kept within four
cubits of his neighbor's dovecote, lest a marten (a
small animal that eats doves) should jump in.
– Mishnah Bava Batra 2:5

Most of us proceed through life minding our
business. But, if we are not careful, our actions
may adversely affect those around us. The
Mishnah, a rabbinic text codified in the year 200
C.E., features many laws about being mindful in
our actions, particularly concerning neighbors. For
instance, a person should be careful where their
ladder is stored so as not to provide access to a
predator of a neighbors' dove habitat. Jewish law
requires that the storage of one's own property be
carefully thought through. This serves as a
reminder to pay attention to your actions because
you may inadvertently negatively affect those
around you. When considering not doing harm in
the world, we must each broaden our scope of
responsibility.

Practice
• Who did you not consider this past year, and as a
result, negative consequences befell that person?
• How might you make amends to them?
• How might you ensure that you are more mindful
of these and other activities in the future so that
you don't negatively impact those around you?

Blessed are You, Creator of the Universe, who commands us to be considerate of, and love, our neighbors.

May you be blessed on your journey over the next 2 days...

Day 28: Planting the Future

כי היכי דשתלי לי אבהתי שתלי נמי לבראי.
Just as my ancestors planted for me, I too am
planting for my descendants.
– Babylonian Talmud, Taanit 23a

A beautiful story in the Talmud tells of a man who approached Honi the Circle Maker while he was in the midst of planting a carob tree. The man asked Honi, "Doesn't a carob tree take 70 years to bear fruit?" "Yes," Honi said. The man retorted, "Well, surely you can't possibly imagine that one day you will taste of its fruit!" Honi waited for a moment before he replied, "Just as my ancestors planted for me, I too am planting for my descendants."

There is an important Jewish value that we have an awareness that everything we do today will have an impact beyond ourselves. Everything, good and bad, will impact the future. Here, Honi reminds us that we should be mindful of this reality.

Additionally, we may apply this principle personally. Everything we do today, every seed we plant, will one day yield fruit. If we would like to be financially secure, equipped to achieve our potential, and healthy in the future, today we may plant the seeds for success by setting up a savings plan, enrolling in a class to acquire new skills, and purchasing a gym membership. By doing things that set yourself up for success, you lead yourself along the path of fulfillment.

Practice
- What fruits do you want to reap in the future?
- What seeds are you planting today— the seeds of discord or the seeds of peace, the seeds of greed or the seeds of generosity, the seeds of love or the seeds of bitterness?
- How might we positively impact our own future and that of those who inherit the world?

Blessed are You, Creator of the Universe, who created the light of Torah.

May you be blessed on your journey over the next day…

Plus One

Day 29: Your Choices Create Reality

וכן כל העולם כולו.
And this can affect the whole world.
– Mishneh Torah, Hilchot Teshuvah 3:1

Rabbi Moshe ben Maimon, also known as
Maimonides, insisted that everyone should
consider themselves to be like a scale equally
balanced having committed the same amount of
vices as virtues. Likewise, each person should
consider the scale of the entire world to be evenly
balanced as well.

Therefore, it stands to reason that every person
should regard each of their actions as capable of
tipping not only their own scale but also the scale
of the entire world towards virtue or vice. That
means that at every given moment, there is an
opportunity to influence one's own state of being
and also that of the entire world. What you do
matters on a personal and global and cosmic scale.

Practice
• Imagine that the world is as evenly balanced as
Maimonides insists that it is; what are you about to
do that will influence the balance? Which way are
you about to tip the scales?
• How can you make sure that what you do in the
next moment, week, month and year will yield a
positive balance for all?
• How will you make certain that the year ahead
will be a positive one?

Blessed are You, Creator of the Universe, who encourages us to choose a good life.

May you be blessed on your journey crossing the threshold into the new year....

About the Author

Rabbi Heather Miller is the founder of Keeping It Sacred (KITS), a center for the exploration of sacred texts and rituals that are accessible, relevant, and empowering.

She was named the 2018 Giant of Justice by CLUE-LA (Clergy and Laity United for Economic Justice), appointed Commissioner on the first-ever Los Angeles County Sheriff's Civilian Oversight Commission in 2016, selected as a Jewish Federation Edah Community Leadership Fellow in 2016, and identified as a Leader to Watch by the Liberty Hill Foundation in 2013.

Rabbi Miller's actions and ideas have been featured in dozens of publications including the NY Times and Jewish Journal. She has served as spiritual leader of several congregations across the United States including the world's first LGBT-founded Jewish synagogue.

Born and raised in an interfaith family in Los Angeles, California, Rabbi Miller received her B.A. from Wellesley College and her M.A. in Hebrew Literature and Rabbinic Ordination from Hebrew Union College–Jewish Institute of Religion. She is a proud member of the Central Conference of American Rabbis, and a Board Member of the Women's Rabbinic Network.

For more information, visit keepingitsacred.com.

CPSIA information can be obtained
at www.ICGtesting.com
Printed in the USA
LVHW031146070721
691986LV00005B/472